THE FABULOUS LOST & FOUND

AND THE LITTLE KOREAN MOUSE

WRITTEN BY MARK PALLIS

ILLUSTRATED BY PETER BAYNTON

NEU WESTEND
— PRESS —

For Emily and Lucy - MP

For Hannah and Skye - PB

THE FABULOUS LOST & FOUND AND THE LITTLE KOREAN MOUSE
Copyright text © 2020 Mark Pallis and Copyright images © 2020 Peter Baynton

Korean Translation by Victoria Eunhye Kim

First Printing, 2020
ISBN: 978-1-913595-11-1
NeuWestendPress.com

THE FABULOUS LOST & FOUND

AND THE LITTLE KOREAN MOUSE

WRITTEN BY MARK PALLIS
ILLUSTRATED BY PETER BAYNTON

NEU WESTEND
— PRESS —

In the middle of the big city is a tiny yellow building. If anyone loses anything, this is where it ends up.

It is called the Lost and Found.

Mr and Mrs Frog keep everything safe, hoping that someday every lost watch and bag and phone and toy and shoe and cheesegrater will find its owner again.

But the shop is very small. And there are so many lost things. It is all quite a squeeze, but still, it's fabulous.

One sunny day, a little mouse walked in.

"Welcome," said Mrs Frog. "What have you lost?"

"모자를 잃어버렸어요," said the mouse.

Mr and Mrs Frog could not speak Korean. They had no idea what the little mouse was saying.

What shall we do? they wondered.

Maybe she's lost an umbrella. Everyone loses an umbrella at least twice, thought Mr Frog.

"Have you lost this?" asked Mr Frog.

"우산이요? 아니요," replied the mouse.

Then Mrs Frog remembered something
that had been handed in a few months ago...

"Is this yours?" Mrs Frog asked, holding up a chunk of cheese.

"치즈요? 냄새나요!" said the mouse.

"Time to put that cheese in the bin dear," said Mr Frog.

"Maybe the word '모자라고요' means coat," said Mr Frog.

"Now where did I put that nice
yellow one?"

"Got it!" said Mr Frog.

"코트요? 아니요, 모자를 잃어버렸어요," said the mouse.

She was starting to feel a bit frustrated.

"We need to keep trying," said Mrs Frog.

목도리도 아니고.

바지도 아니고.

긴팔 옷 아니고.

선글라스도 아니고.

신발도 아니에요.

"모자를 잃어버렸어요," said the mouse.

자전거 두 개도 아니고.

컴퓨터도 아니고.

책 세 권도 아니고.

바나나 네 개도 아니고.

열쇠 다섯 개도 아니에요.

It was no good. A fat wet tear rolled
down the mouse's cheek.

"How about a nice cup of tea?" asked Mrs Frog kindly.

"차를 좋아해요. 감사합니다," replied the mouse. They sat together, sipping their tea and all feeling a bit sad.

Suddenly, the mouse realised she could try pointing.

She pointed at her head.

"모자라고요!" she said.

"I've got it!" exclaimed Mrs Frog, leaping up.

"A wig of course!" said Mrs Frog.

"가발이 아니에요," said the mouse.

빨간색도 아니고.

금색도 아니고.

갈색도 아니고.

초록색도 아니고.

화려한 색도 아니에요.

"What about this?"
asked Mr Frog, pulling back
a curtain.

"모자라고요!"
exclaimed the mouse.

"Ah, so '모자라고요' means
hat. Wonderful!" Mr and
Mrs Frog cheered.

너무 길어요.

너무 작아요.

너무 딱 맞아요.

너무 커요.

"One hat left," said
Mrs Frog, reaching all
the way to the back of the
cupboard.

"It couldn't be this
old thing, could it?"

"제 모자예요.

모자를 찾았어요!

감사합니다," said the mouse.

And just like that, the mouse found her hat.

"안녕히 계세요," said the mouse, as she skipped away.

"I wonder who will come tomorrow?" said Mr Frog.
Mrs Frog put her arm around him.

"I don't know," she replied, giving him a squeeze, "but
whoever it is, we'll do our best to help."

LEARNING TO LOVE LANGUAGES

An additional language opens a child's mind, broadens their horizons and enriches their emotional life. Research has shown that the time between a child's birth and their sixth or seventh birthday is a "golden period" when they are most receptive to new languages. This is because they have an in-built ability to distinguish the sounds they hear and make sense of them. The Story-powered Language Learning Method taps into these natural abilities.

HOW THE STORY-POWERED LANGUAGE LEARNING METHOD WORKS

We create an emotionally engaging and funny story for children and adults to enjoy together, just like any other picture book. Studies show that social interaction, like enjoying a book together, is critical in language learning.

Through the story, we introduce a relatable character who speaks only in the new language. This helps build empathy and a positive attitude towards people who speak different languages. These are both important aspects in laying the foundations for lasting language acquisition in a child's life.

As the story progresses, the child naturally works with the characters to discover the meaning of a wide range of fun new words. Strategic use of humour ensures that this subconscious learning is rewarded with laughter; the child feels good and the first seeds of a lifelong love of languages are sown.

For more information and free downloads visit www.neuwestendpress.com

모자를 잃어버렸어요	I've lost my hat	화려한	multicoloured
우산	umbrella	아니요	no
치즈	cheese	내 모자	my hat
냄새나요	it stinks	너무 길어요	too tall
코트	coat	너무 커요	too big
목도리	scarf	너무 작아요	too small
바지	trousers	너무 딱 맞아요	too tight
선글라스	sunglasses	제 모자를 찾았어요	I've found my hat
긴팔 옷	long sleeved top	정말 감사합니다	thank you very much
신발	shoes	안녕히 계세요	goodbye
하나	one		
둘	two		
셋	three		
넷	four		
다섯	five		
컴퓨터	computer		
책	book		
열쇠	key		
자전거	bicycle		
차를 좋아해요	I love tea		
감사합니다	thank you		
가발	wig		
빨간색	red		
금발	blond		
갈색	brown		
초록색	green		

THE WORLD OF
THE FABULOUS LOST & FOUND

THIS STORY IS ALSO AVAILABLE IN...

FRENCH

SPANISH

ITALIAN

CZECH

WELSH

CHINESE

GERMAN

HEBREW

SWEDISH

POLISH

SLOVAKIAN

VIETNAMESE

LATIN

PORTUGUESE

...AND MANY MORE LANGUAGES!

ENJOYED IT?
WRITE A REVIEW AND
LET US KNOW!

@MARK_PALLIS ON TWITTER
WWW.MARKPALLIS.COM

@PETERBAYNTON ON INSTAGRAM
WWW.PETERBAYNTON.COM